*It must be bad enough
to stumble upon a murder.
I had stumbled upon a
secret society of murderers
with a King for a crony man.*

Edmund Morel, upon discovering
King Leopold II's system of
forced labor in the Congo

This book is for Richard and Estie.

Photographs © 2008: Art Resource, NY: 24 (Adoc-photos), 89 top (E. Morel/The New York Public Library), 89 bottom right (Musee de l'Homme, Paris, France), 90 bottom (Snark), 70, 88 top, 90 center, 91 top left, 97 (The New York Public Library); Bridgeman Art Library International Ltd., London/New York: 82 (Archives Nationales, Centre des Archives d'Outre-Mer), 44 (Bibliotheque de L'Arsenal, Paris, France), 89 bottom left (Charles Louis Girault/Private Collection); Corbis Images: 54, 76 (Bettmann), 80 (Grand Tour), 66, 91 bottom (Hulton-Deutsch Collection); Getty Images: 10 (W. & D. Downey/Hulton Archive), 31 (Geruzet Brothers/Hulton Archive), 86 center (Hulton Archive), 62 (Martin & Osa Johnson Safari Museum), 90 top (Kean Collection), 105 (Stock Montage), 107 (Topical Press Agency), 112 (Roger Viollet); Mary Evans Picture Library: 19, 39, 47, 87 top, 88 bottom; The Granger Collection, New York: 36, 52, 64, 86 top, 86 bottom, 87 bottom left, 87 bottom right, 91 top right.

Library of Congress Cataloging-in-Publication Data

Olson, Tod.
Leopold II : butcher of the Congo / Tod Olson.
p. cm. — (A wicked history)
Includes bibliographical references and index.
ISBN-13: 978-0-531-18552-0 (lib. bdg.) 978-0-531-20501-3 (pbk.)
ISBN-10: 0-531-18552-4 (lib. bdg.) 0-531-20501-0 (pbk.)
1. Léopold II, King of the Belgians, 1835-1909. 2. Congo (Democratic Republic)—History—To 1908. 3. Belgium—Kings and rulers—Biography. I. Title.
DH671.O45 2008
967.51'022092—dc22
[B]
2007034951

Illustrations by XNR Productions, Inc.: 4, 5, 8, 9
Cover art, page 8 inset by Mark Summers
Chapter art by Raphael Montoliu

Tod Olson, Series Editor
Marie O'Neill, Art Director
Allicette Torres, Cover Design
SimonSays Design!, Book Design and Production

© 2008 Scholastic Inc.

3 4 5 6 7 8 9 10 R 17 16 15 14 13 12 11 10

Leopold II

Butcher of
the Congo

TOD OLSON

Franklin Watts
An Imprint of Scholastic Inc.
New York   Toronto   London   Auckland   Sydney
Mexico City   New Delhi   Hong Kong
Danbury, Connecticut

The World of Leopold II

Leopold II was king of Belgium, a small country in Europe.
But he was obsessed with Africa's Congo region, where he ruled
an area more than 70 times the size of his homeland.

KEY

A Explorer H. M. Stanley embarked on a voyage to follow the Congo River to the Atlantic.

B King Leopold met the explorer Verney Lovett Cameron in May 1876. Cameron told him about the riches of the Congo.

C Leopold hosted the Geographical Conference in 1876 in Brussels. He claimed his goal was to wipe out the slave trade in Africa.

D In 1879, under Leopold's direction, Stanley began work on a road from Boma to Stanley Pool.

E In November 1884, the Berlin Conference met to divide up Africa.

F In 1885, Leopold's governor-general moved into a mansion in Boma. In 1904, Roger Casement completed his fact-finding trip of the Congo Free State here. He then wrote a report listing Leopold's crimes. Four years later, there was a ceremony in this village, as the colony was taken from Leopold.

—— Stanley's exploration of the Congo, 1874–1877

Map shows boundaries of 1890.

N

miles
0   250   500

0   250 500
kilometers

TABLE OF CONTENTS

A Wicked Web

A look at the allies and enemies of Leopold II.

Leopold's Family and Friends

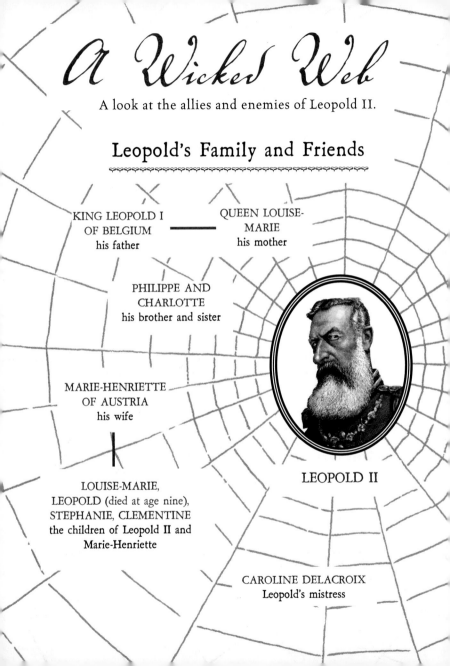

KING LEOPOLD I OF BELGIUM
his father

QUEEN LOUISE-MARIE
his mother

PHILIPPE AND CHARLOTTE
his brother and sister

MARIE-HENRIETTE OF AUSTRIA
his wife

LOUISE-MARIE, LEOPOLD (died at age nine), **STEPHANIE, CLEMENTINE**
the children of Leopold II and Marie-Henriette

LEOPOLD II

CAROLINE DELACROIX
Leopold's mistress

Explorers

꧂꧂꧂꧂꧂꧂꧂꧂꧂꧂

DAVID LIVINGSTONE
first European to see Victoria
Falls, in Africa

HENRY MORTON STANLEY
explored the Congo and built
the early settlements of
Leopold's colony

VERNEY LOVETT CAMERON
crossed Africa south of the Congo
River; told Leopold about the
area's riches

Leopold's Opponents and Critics

꧂꧂꧂꧂꧂꧂꧂꧂꧂꧂꧂꧂꧂꧂꧂꧂꧂꧂꧂꧂꧂꧂꧂꧂꧂꧂꧂꧂꧂

EDMUND MOREL
founded the Congo Reform
Association, which exposed
Leopold's crimes to the world

ROGER CASEMENT
British representative whose
report on abuses in the Congo
helped bring about the downfall
of the Congo Free State

**GEORGE WASHINGTON
WILLIAMS**
journalist who visited the
Congo in 1890; first person to
publicly criticize Leopold II

JOHN MURPHY
Baptist missionary who told
British newspapers about abuses
in the Congo

LEOPOLD II, King of the Belgians
and King Sovereign of the Congo Free State (1835–1909)

Congo Free State, 1890

DURING THE SPRING of 1890, American journalist George Washington Williams made his way slowly up the Congo River into the heart of Africa. It wasn't an easy trip. The Congo rushes down its final path to the ocean in huge waterfalls and foaming rapids. No boat could make it past the white water. After traveling 60 miles on a steamship, Williams had to walk for 200 miles on a rough dirt road. Only then could he board another steamship to make the rest of the journey.

The breeze on the river must have been a relief. The weather was steaming hot and damp. Only the wind and the wood fire in the steamship boiler kept the mosquitoes away. The ship traveled 30 miles a day. It stopped in the evening so its African crew could cut more wood for the boiler.

Nearly everyone Williams saw in the Congo had dark skin like his own. But every so often the steamship stopped at a tiny collection of huts. White Europeans, often dressed in bright white suits, came out to greet him.

Williams thought that these little settlements, called stations, were the beginnings of civilization in the Congo. He had high hopes for them. Just 25 years earlier, Williams had fought to end slavery in his own country's Civil War. Now, he had a dream. He wanted to bring African Americans back to Africa to help their sisters and brothers. And the Congo Free State seemed like a promising place to start.

One man more than any other was responsible for this new nation. He was Leopold II, King of the Belgians. The Congo was Leopold's colony. It belonged not to Belgium, but to the king himself. From his tiny country in Europe, he ruled nearly a million square miles of Africa. Yet he had never set foot on the continent.

In 1889, Williams had met Leopold and liked him very much. Williams interviewed the king for an American newspaper. Leopold received the African-American man at his palace in Brussels. The king told the journalist that he had started a great and noble project in the Congo.

Leopold claimed he was fighting to end slavery there. He wanted to open the land to trade with the rest of the world. He would educate Africans and train them to build their economy. Eventually they would run their own country. "What I do there is done as a Christian duty to the poor African," Leopold told Williams. "I do not wish to have one Belgian franc back of all the money I have expended."

Williams was charmed. He wrote home to his newspaper that Leopold was "one of the noblest sovereigns in the world." The king treated his subjects with "wisdom, mercy, and justice," Williams said.

Then he left for Africa to see Leopold's work for himself. Months later, as he steamed up the Congo River, he began to think he had been dead wrong about the "noble" king.

Along the river, Williams found no evidence that the white newcomers were helping the Africans. He saw no schools or hospitals. The stations were the only sign of Leopold's efforts. And they seemed to be little more than military bases. The white station chiefs demanded food and elephant tusks from the Africans. The food provided meals for the station chiefs and their African soldiers. The tusks were sent down river to be sold in Europe for ivory.

The white men ruled without mercy or justice. If the Africans refused to bring food or ivory, they were punished harshly. The station chiefs and their black soldiers burned rebel villages. They chained people by the neck to make them work. At one point, Williams met two white officers on a steamer. The officers bet on whether or not they could shoot an African who was walking on shore. In three shots, the African man was dead.

Williams's trip up the Congo made him enraged. In July 1890, he stopped at a station 1,000 miles upriver from the ocean. He sat down to write a letter to Leopold. The letter charged the king with "crimes against humanity." Leopold was not getting rid of slavery in the Congo, Williams claimed. He was creating it. The king, Williams said, had as much right to rule the Congo "as I have to be the Commander-in-Chief of the Belgian Army."

Williams did what he could to tell the world about what he had seen. He sent his letter to be printed as a pamphlet. He wrote the president of the United States, Grover Cleveland, about the Congo.

His efforts caused a minor scandal. But Williams didn't live long enough to press the issue. In 1891 he died of a lung disease in London.

Leopold II was once again free to rule the Congo as he pleased.

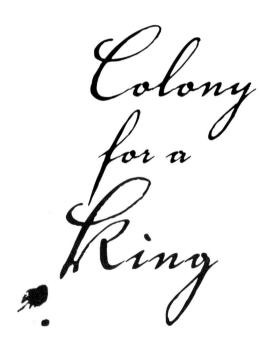

PART 1

Colony
for a
King

CHAPTER 1

Growing Up Royal

The heir to the Belgian throne is
A DISAPPOINTMENT
TO THE KING.

LEOPOLD II WAS BORN IN 1835, 55 years
before Williams's voyage to Africa. His home was a
sprawling palace at Laeken, just outside the Belgian
capital of Brussels.

As a boy, the future king of the Congo hardly
seemed like a natural leader. Young Leopold was
thin, awkward, and sickly. His father often called him
"odd," "funny," and "unruly." His own mother, Queen
Louise-Marie of Orléans, said his huge nose made him

YOUNG LEOPOLD WAS A DISAPPOINTMENT
to his parents. They preferred their daughter, Charlotte (right),
and youngest son, Philippe (center).

look deformed and "birdlike." Both parents liked their
younger son, Philippe, better than Leopold.

The royal couple put a Belgian army colonel in
charge of the boys and their sister Charlotte. The
colonel ran their lives like a military camp. The

children had a schedule for each day. It began at 6:30 A.M. and ended at 5:00 P.M. They got three hours off for meals and spent the rest of the time studying.

Their mother took over in the evening. She made them study for another hour before bedtime. Every month she tested them to see how they were doing. If they passed, she gave them reading material as a prize. Philippe and Charlotte usually went to bed with brand-new books. Leopold often got nothing. "I was very disturbed to see," his mother wrote to him once, ". . . that you had again been so lazy and that your exercises had been so bad and careless."

A year after she wrote that note, Leopold's mother got sick. Near the end of her life, she lay in bed in great pain. Her three children gathered around her. She kissed each one of them before she died. Leopold was just 15.

After his mother's death, Leopold grew even more quiet and awkward. He got no comfort from his father. The king used his secretary to pass messages to his son. The family rarely even ate meals together. Young Leopold had to make appointments to see his father.

The king, however, knew his son well. He told an aide once that he had seen a fox that reminded him of Leopold. The fox had been crossing a stream step by step. After each step, it tested the water with a paw to see how deep it was. That was Leopold, the king said. He was "subtle and sly" and determined to get what he wanted.

And there was one thing Leopold seemed to want badly. Despite his bad study habits, Leopold wanted to learn about the world. As a teenager, he liked to talk about politics. Most of all he loved to study geography.

Leopold began to make friends among the government ministers who worked for his father. He begged them for information about the world beyond Belgium. Best of all, he got maps from them. In the palace at Laeken and in the king's offices in Brussels, he studied his treasures. And he began to develop a picture of the world in 1850.

Tiny Belgium was surrounded by its much older and more powerful neighbors—Prussia (Germany), Austria-Hungary, Holland, France, Spain, and England. Since the 1500s, these major powers had been claiming land around the globe. They had colonies in Latin America, Asia, and the Pacific. Ships brought European settlers to the colonies and returned home with valuable goods such as tea, tobacco, or gold.

Belgium, however, had no colonies and no part in this rich trade. No ships sailed into Belgian harbors with loads of exotic goods. Young, adventurous Belgians had no overseas missions to undertake. They had only Belgium, which was no bigger than the state of Maryland. Already, it was beginning to seem too small to Leopold.

CHAPTER 2

Out of Town

THE PRINCE GETS MARRIED
and goes on the road.

IN 1853, LEOPOLD TURNED 18. His father decided it was time for him to marry. And like most royal children, Leopold didn't get to choose his wife. Princes and princesses did not marry for love. They married to make political deals. Leopold's father wanted the powerful Austro-Hungarian Empire as an ally. So he found Leopold an Austrian archduchess to marry.

In the spring of 1853, Leopold went to Vienna to meet his bride. The two didn't have much in common. The archduchess, Marie-Henriette, was

LEOPOLD AND HIS BRIDE DIDN'T HAVE MUCH IN COMMON.
Marie-Henriette loved horses, parties, and the arts.
Leopold cared only for war and politics.

a tomboy. She loved horses, music, books, and art. She had a loud laugh and a lively personality. Leopold, on the other hand, had almost no sense of humor. He could talk for hours about war and politics. But he had little interest in anything else. One Austrian lady said it looked like a marriage "between a stable-boy and a nun." Leopold, she explained, was the nun.

The prince and the archduchess got married in August, just three months after they met. The people of Brussels were treated to a parade and a concert. Fireworks exploded over the city to celebrate the wedding.

In private, there was no spark between the newlyweds. Marie-Henriette left her family behind and moved into the palace at Laeken. Leopold rarely spoke to her. She tried to make friends with Leopold's sister, Charlotte. But Charlotte ignored her as well. So, Marie-Henriette went riding alone. In the evening she went to concerts.

Leopold, meanwhile, pressured his father to let him travel. When the king refused, Leopold got his doctors to say that a warm climate would improve his health. He also asked his father's secretary to plead his case. "I have . . . only one desire, and that is to learn as much as possible about the world and its peoples," he told the secretary.

For several years, that's exactly what the prince did. Leopold traveled to Turkey, Palestine, Italy, Greece, and Egypt. He went to Romania and the Balkans. He visited Ceylon, India, Burma, Singapore, and Sumatra. He met with the Turkish sultan, the Egyptian khedive, and dozens of European princes.

The king grumbled that Leopold was "flying about in an absurd manner." He accused his son of faking illness as an excuse to travel. In 1859, he finally insisted that Leopold stay home. Marie-Henriette was pregnant with their second child. If not for his father, Leopold would have been in Sweden or Norway for the birth of his son.

During his travels, Leopold became convinced of one thing: Belgium had to have a colony. England and Spain set fine examples, he felt. Their overseas empires created prestige and power. They also created wealth.

A colony would give Belgian companies new land to develop. Native people would work cheaply—or for free. Gold, silver, ivory, and other valuable raw materials might be found. If only the Belgian people would wake up and realize the value of overseas expansion. Then, he wrote, "Belgium would become one of the richest countries in the world."

Leopold became obsessed with turning tiny Belgium into a great power. He gave speeches in Parliament. He helped write pamphlets. He gathered mountains of information. In 1862 he spent a month in Spain studying exactly how much money the Spanish had made from their empire. He sent his closest aide, a man named Brialmont, to Paris to do research. He asked Brialmont to buy atlases in London. He wore him out asking for facts and figures. Leopold, Brialmont said, "takes me for a statistical office."

The Belgian people and their representatives in Parliament didn't share Leopold's dreams of overseas conquest. Belgium had no navy and few merchant ships, they pointed out. How could it take advantage of a colony an ocean away? Besides, Belgium had always stayed neutral in disputes around the world. Joining the race for land around the globe might lead to conflicts with the great powers.

Leopold shrugged off these objections. And he went shopping for a colony. He tried to buy a lake near the Nile River from the Egyptians. He negotiated with the British for their piece of Borneo. He looked into Fiji in the Pacific and Formosa off the coast of China. He investigated a province in Argentina and an island in the Uruguay River. "Who owns this island?" he wrote to an aide. "Could one buy it?"

But every deal Leopold tried to make fell through. He could only watch while other countries slowly added to their empires. On Africa's west coast, the French built bases in Senegal. The British began to move into Nigeria. Europeans seemed to be grabbing all the "unoccupied" land on earth. "The time has come for us to spread ourselves outward," Leopold said. "We cannot afford to lose more time."

In May 1865, Leopold returned from a trip through Asia and the Pacific. He found his father ill and getting worse by the day. The king spent his last weeks in his room at Laeken. A pianist played music for him. An aide read him novels. On December 10, 1865, he died.

At age 30, Leopold became King of the Belgians.

CHAPTER 3

King of the Belgians

Leopold takes over a nation—but IT JUST ISN'T ENOUGH.

ON DECEMBER 17, 1865, Leopold prepared to be crowned King of the Belgians. He dressed in a general's uniform. He mounted a horse and rode in a great parade from Laeken to the capital. He refused to let his wife and children enter the city with him. But their absence did not ruin the mood. The people of Brussels welcomed their new king. They waved handkerchiefs as Leopold rode through the streets.

LEOPOLD ENTERED BRUSSELS TO BE CROWNED KING of the Belgians in 1865. He refused to let his family join his parade.

They threw flowers at his feet. In Parliament, Leopold was sworn in with great hope for the future.

The future, however, did not look bright for the royal family.

Leopold's nine-year-old son became ill with pneumonia. He died in January 1869. Leopold was devastated. At the funeral, the king fell to his knees in front of the coffin and wept.

Leopold's marriage gave him no comfort. He and Marie-Henriette grew even further apart after their son's death. They would have two more children, both daughters. But they barely spoke to each other.

Leopold still had grand plans for Belgium. But the Belgian people took little interest in them. Parliament refused to let the king use government funds for his colonial schemes. And Leopold grew frustrated. "I am King of a small country and small-minded people," he complained.

But Leopold was not one to give up easily. He tried his best to escape Belgium whenever he could. And he resolved that if Belgium didn't want a colony, he would simply buy it himself.

Leopold went shopping again. He tried to buy land in China. He asked the Dutch to sell their portion of Borneo. He talked with Portugal about land in Timor, Mozambique, and Angola. He negotiated with Spain for part of the Philippines. He looked into New Guinea, French Indochina, and two islands off the coast of Turkey. One by one, the deals fell through.

But one place on the globe still seemed promising: Africa.

CHAPTER 4

A New World

European adventurers begin exploring Africa—AND LEOPOLD TAKES NOTICE.

BY THE LATE 1800s, Africa's coastline was well mapped by Europeans. White traders had been buying and stealing slaves there for 300 years. But they rarely traveled inland. Most of the continent and its hundreds of tribal groups were still unknown to Europeans.

That was finally beginning to change. Since the early 1850s, white explorers had been racing to find the source of the Nile River. In the process, they uncovered a land full of wonders. They found the snow-capped Mount Kilimanjaro in Kenya. They stumbled across the longest freshwater lake in the world, Lake Tanganyika. An English doctor named David Livingstone became the first European to see the mile-wide Victoria Falls.

The explorers became celebrities when they returned. Newspapers ran front-page stories about their adventures. Many of the explorers went on tour to lecture and show off souvenirs from their travels. They told tales of fearsome animals and violent tribal chiefs. One French explorer brought home gorilla skeletons to show at his lectures. The beasts, he claimed, kidnapped women and dragged them off into the jungle.

In 1871, one explorer had all of Europe talking. His name was Henry Morton Stanley. That spring, an American newspaper sent Stanley on a mission into central Africa. David Livingstone had been wandering there for five years. No one had heard from him. Stanley's job was to find him.

Stanley completed his mission, but it nearly killed him. By the end of October, he was sick and hungry. One day he sat down to carve a desperate message into the bark of a tree: "Starving. HMS."

Stanley struggled on, following a rumor that an old white man with a grey beard was living in a village called Ujiji. Stanley stumbled into the village. He found the white man in a crowd of

ACCORDING TO NEWS REPORTS, explorer David Livingstone was lost in central Africa. Fellow explorer Henry Morton Stanley went to rescue him. Livingstone, however, did not want to be rescued.

Africans. Stanley walked up to him and said, "Dr. Livingstone, I presume?"

Livingstone, it turned out, did not need to be rescued. He stayed in Africa. Yet Stanley returned to a hero's welcome in Europe. He went on tour to boast about his accomplishments. He wrote articles and published a book. *How I Found Livingstone* became a bestseller.

Back at the palace in Laeken, King Leopold followed Stanley's story closely in the newspapers. Lands that Europeans had never seen before were finally being explored. How exciting it must have been to a man who loved to learn about the world. And how much more exciting it would be if a piece of that land could someday be his.

CHAPTER 5

Into Africa

Stanley goes exploring, while Leopold
MAKES PLANS FROM AFAR.

IN 1874, LEOPOLD'S ATTENTION once again
turned to Africa. Henry Morton Stanley was making
preparations to cross the entire continent from east
to west. His goal was to find the source of the Congo
River and follow it all the way to the Atlantic Ocean.

In November 1874, Stanley and a small army of
travelers left Zanzibar on Africa's east coast. They
headed west into the jungle. There were 360 travelers,
nearly all of them black. The line stretched for half a
mile through the jungle.

Most of the people in the party were porters, hired by Stanley. They carried heavy loads on their backs. A 40-foot boat, broken down into five sections, swung suspended from long poles. Many of the men had rifles. Others carried backpacks stuffed with goods to be traded for food along the way.

AFRICANS PROVIDED THE MUSCLE for Henry Morton Stanley's expedition in central Africa. Here, porters carve a dugout canoe as Stanley watches.

The entire expedition carried 16,000 pounds of supplies. They would need every ounce. They had a 7,000-mile journey ahead of them, a journey that would change the history of Africa forever.

The last reports of Stanley's voyage came from Zanzibar. Then the explorer vanished into the jungle, beyond communication with Europeans.

Leopold kept track of Stanley as long as he could. Africa had caught the king's eye. And as always, he was ready to do his research. He wrote to an aide, "I intend to find out discreetly if there is anything to be done in Africa."

In May 1876, King Leopold went to London to meet an explorer named Verney Lovett Cameron. Cameron had just crossed Africa south of the Congo River. He told Leopold what he had reported in the newspapers. It was a land of "unspeakable riches." The earth was rich with coal, gold, silver, copper, and iron. And the rivers made it easy to transport people and goods.

Leopold listened with great interest. Already he had a plan. The Belgians still wanted no part of his colonial schemes. And other European nations were beginning to compete for land in Africa. If Leopold appeared to be grabbing part of Africa for himself, the great powers would object. Suppose, however, that he organized a group of important explorers and geographers from all over Europe. And suppose he told everyone that the goal of this group was not to take land for profit—but to help the Africans. Who could object to such a project?

In a matter of months, Leopold organized a Geographical Conference in Brussels. In September 1876, 24 foreign guests arrived in the Belgian capital. The king greeted them personally in his palace.

Leopold opened the conference with a speech. He had considered carefully how he would announce their mission. But this time, the European slave trade had died out on the west coast of Africa. But Arab traders kept the business alive and well in the east. Activists in Europe were furious that the evil business was still thriving there. The members of the Geographical Conference, Leopold announced, would launch a crusade to wipe out the slave trade.

In the days that followed, members of the group studied maps. They planned a series of bases along the Congo River. Each base would be staffed by scientists, artisans, and doctors. Their job would be to study the environment and teach the Africans. They also made plans to share the bases with military units that would fight slavery and make peace among the tribes of the region.

Before the delegates left they formed the International African Association. (Its initials in French were AIA.) They designed a flag for themselves—a gold star on a blue background. Leopold was chosen to be the group's chairman.

The king said nothing during the conference about his desire to own a colony. He insisted that he had no interest in money or power. All he wanted was to help the Africans, he claimed.

Privately, Leopold spoke with a little more honesty. Not long after the conference ended, he wrote that he wanted the Congo for himself. He was eager, he said, to get his hands on "a slice of this magnificent African cake."

The man who could help Leopold the most was missing from the king's conference. In September 1876, Henry Stanley was still lost in Africa. No one had heard from him in months.

SLAVE TRADE

AFRICAN TRIBES HAD BEEN TRADING SLAVES FOR YEARS. But Europeans turned the slave trade into one of the most brutal crimes in history.

A GROUP of African slaves, chained at the neck.

The demand for slaves came mostly from the Americas. Europeans began settling there in the early 1500s. They wanted people to work the mines and harvest sugar, tobacco, cotton, and coffee.

Whites arrived on the West African coast at around the same time. They began buying Africans in exchange for cloth, guns, tools, jewelry, or liquor.

By the mid-1500s, 20,000 Africans a year were crowded onto ships and sent across the Atlantic. A century later, nearly 60,000 slaves a year made the trip.

The trade finally stopped in the 1860s. But by this time, Arab slavers had arrived in central Africa. Each year they sent about 30,000 Africans to the Middle East.

CHAPTER 6

Mr. Stanley, I Presume

The explorer returns and MEETS THE KING.

ABOUT A YEAR AFTER Leopold's Geographical Conference, in August 1877, Henry Morton Stanley made contact with the European world again. He sent four African men to deliver a desperate message to Boma, a tiny village on the Congo River. Boma lay just 50 miles from Africa's west coast.

Stanley's letter was addressed to "any gentleman who speaks English." It began, "Dear Sir, I have arrived at this place from Zanzibar with 115 souls—men, women, and children. We are now in a state of . . . starvation."

The letter went on to beg for help. The travelers desperately needed rice and grain. Their leader asked for "such little luxuries as coffee, tea, sugar, and biscuits." The supplies must arrive within two days, he said. If not, he would "have a fearful time of it among the dying."

The letter was signed "H. M. Stanley." In case his name was not enough, Stanley added a postscript. "I am the person that discovered Livingstone in 1871."

Stanley got his supplies just in time. He gathered his people and finished his journey to the coast. He had traveled 7,000 miles in 999 days. And he had done something no white man had ever done before. He had followed the Congo nearly its entire length to the sea.

The journey had taken its toll. Stanley arrived 60 pounds lighter than when he started. And he was one of the lucky ones. Half the party had died along the way.

Stanley made the long journey back to England, where he went on tour. He spoke at dinners and in lecture halls. People often stood and cheered. But not everyone was thrilled with the explorer's march across Africa.

Stanley had led his expedition like a military mission. When tribal chiefs tried to keep him from passing, he opened fire. His riflemen used elephant guns with exploding bullets. Their opponents fought with spears and bows and arrows. Stanley boasted that

STANLEY THREATENS TO SHOOT A PORTER if he drops a box in the river. Stanley treated his porters terribly. Half of them died during the journey across Africa.

he destroyed 28 large towns and 60 to 80 villages on his way across Africa.

He was also ruthless with his own people. He called his porters "faithless, lying, and thievish." He whipped them when they got drunk. Rumor had it that he had kicked a porter to death.

Still, Stanley bragged about his exploits. He wrote another bestseller. In it he insisted that his discoveries had great economic value. Dozens of rivers flowed into the Congo, he pointed out. The system of waterways made it easy to move goods around an area of a million square miles. "This river," he concluded, "will be the grand highway of commerce to west central Africa."

That was exactly what Leopold wanted to hear. For months, he had waited for news of Stanley's return. Now he couldn't wait to meet the man. He sent messengers to invite the explorer to Brussels. Leopold wanted the Congo, and Stanley was going to help him take it.

But Leopold knew he had to be careful. If the British knew he wanted to take over part of Africa, they would certainly try to stop him. The British and the other powers were working on their own plans to control parts of Africa. They could not afford to occupy every inch of the continent. But they didn't want any of it closed off to foreign trade. The major powers wanted to make sure that the land stayed open to their merchants and businessmen.

Any attempt to grab land in Africa would be watched closely. Leopold told the Belgian minister in London to keep his plans secret. The public should think that he simply wanted Stanley to explore the area.

But Leopold was interested in more than exploration. In June 1878, Stanley arrived in Belgium to see the king. Leopold received him at the Royal Palace in Brussels. The two men worked out a deal. The king offered Stanley a salary worth $300,000 a year in today's money. In return, Stanley agreed to go back to Africa. His task, according to Leopold: "Set up a base on the Congo and from there, spread out in all directions."

By this time, the group set up at Leopold's conference, the AIA, had dissolved. Leopold set up a new organization that sounded a lot like the old one. He called it the International Association of the Congo. The organization used the flag of the old AIA. There was one big difference: The International Association of the Congo was not international at all. It was controlled by Leopold and Leopold alone.

The king's plan was underway. Stanley would quietly build a road and stations in the Congo under the "international" flag. In fact, the stations would belong to Leopold. Eventually, the king reasoned, the world would get used to his presence in the Congo. Then, the slice of "magnificent cake" would be his.

CHAPTER 7

Race for the Congo

Can the king of tiny Belgium
convince the world to let him
RULE A MILLION SQUARE
MILES IN AFRICA?

IN FEBRUARY 1879, LEOPOLD AND STANLEY
put their plan into action. Everything went ahead with great
secrecy. Leopold was racing the French, the Portuguese,
and the British for control of the Congo. He did not want
his rivals to know how quickly he was moving.

Stanley sneaked aboard a steamship bound for
Africa. He signed his name "M. Henri" to avoid
suspicion. Leopold sent 12 Europeans to help him.

Each employee had to sign an agreement promising not to talk about the mission.

By August, Stanley was back in the Congo with 80 armed men from Zanzibar. He had an enormous task at hand. He had to carve a 200-mile road out of the thick jungle from Boma to Stanley Pool.

Stanley had definitely exaggerated when he called the Congo a "grand highway." From Boma to Stanley Pool, the water was a mass of swirling

PORTERS STEER STANLEY'S CANOE BETWEEN ROCKS
in the rapids of the Congo River. Contrary to Stanley's claims,
much of the river was not navigable.

rapids. Long sections of river were nearly impassable. Travelers had to carry their boats around rapids to reach calmer waters.

Stanley's task was to make that job easier. He started by sending messengers to the tribal chiefs in the area. They gathered for a meeting. With his Zanzibari soldiers standing by, Stanley asked the chiefs for permission to build his road. The chiefs bargained for a few hundred dollars worth of cloth. In the end, they agreed to let Stanley begin building Leopold's empire.

With a crew of 200 African laborers, Stanley got to work. His workers hacked a trail through the jungle. They built log bridges over streams. They blasted their way through cliffs and boulders. They hauled 600 tons of boats, machinery, and lumber slowly up river.

It was grueling work. In a year and half Stanley's crew had built just 52 miles of road.

In Belgium, Leopold was anxious. He sent a steady stream of messages to Stanley telling him to work faster. Stanley answered with frustration. With more laborers, he could make better progress, he said. But he could not attract more workers. The Congolese had no need for the wages he offered them.

Early in 1882, Stanley finally finished his road. By this time, he was so ill that he had to leave for Europe. When he arrived in Belgium, Leopold told him to turn around. His work was just beginning.

UNDER STANLEY'S DIRECTION, African porters carved their way through central Africa. It took three years to build a 200-mile road from Boma to Stanley Pool.

So far, Stanley had simply asked the local chiefs for permission to build his road. That was not enough for Leopold. French explorers had moved into the Congo region from the north. It was time to buy the land outright, before it all belonged to France. "Surely, Mr. Stanley," Leopold told the explorer, "you cannot think of leaving me now, just when I need you most."

At the end of the year, Stanley dragged himself back to Africa. In grass huts and forest clearings he met with the chiefs of the Congo. Most of these men had never seen the written word before. Still, one by one, they signed away their land. In return some got used army uniforms. Some received a few pieces of cloth each month. Still others got bottles of gin.

The process happened peacefully for the most part. But by this time, Stanley had 1,000 rifles, a dozen small cannons, and four machine guns. To many tribal chiefs, making an "x" on a piece of paper must have seemed like the only choice.

In the summer of 1884, Stanley came back to Europe. He reported to Leopold that his work was done. He had finished the road. He had built stations along the Congo for 1,500 miles. He had 400 treaties in hand, signed by 2,000 chiefs. Now, Leopold had to convince the rest of the world that the Congo should be his.

The king began a public relations campaign. He told senators from the United States that his people in the Congo were there to study the region and give "aid to travelers." The plan was to educate the Africans and eventually to end slavery. Leopold promised the British minister in Belgium that he had no desire to make money in the Congo. He told the Germans that the Africans would eventually govern themselves.

Not everyone believed Leopold. But one by one, the powerful nations accepted his hold over the Congo. Belgium was, after all, a weak nation. Germany, France, and England did not want one of their stronger rivals controlling that large a portion of Africa.

In November 1884, the major powers of Europe gathered in Berlin for a conference on Africa. The delegates sat around a horseshoe-shaped table. In front of them lay a huge map of Africa. For four months, they argued over which part of Africa belonged to whom. Stanley was there to plead Leopold's case. And by February, Leopold had what he wanted. His representatives promised to allow all nations to trade freely in the Congo. In return, the great powers gave Leopold control over the area.

Now, there was no longer any question who ruled the Congo. The Belgian Parliament had no control over it. The International Association of the Congo had quietly disappeared. In May 1885, Leopold became the sole ruler of the Congo. He called his new kingdom the Congo Free State. It was as big as the United States east of the Mississippi.

Leopold considered calling himself the "emperor" of the Congo. He settled for "king sovereign."

PART 2

Secrets
of the
Congo

CHAPTER 8

೪೪೪೪೪೪೪೪೪೪೪೪೪

King of the Congo

Leopold begins to
BUILD A NATION.

IN 1885, LEOPOLD WAS 50 YEARS OLD. He had spent his entire adult life trying to acquire a colony. Now, he had one that was bigger than he had dreamed. But the work was just beginning. And Leopold went at it with tremendous energy.

At home in Belgium, he woke every morning at 5:00 A.M. He drank a glass of warm water and went for a walk. By 6:00 he was reading letters, many of them about the Congo Free State. At 7:30 his secretary arrived to write out the king's replies. Breakfast was a half-dozen eggs, bread, and a whole jar of jam. Then Leopold dragged an aide on a two-hour hike around the grounds. While they walked, the king gave orders and dictated letters. During lunch, Leopold talked politics over steak and vegetables. Then he left for his office in Brussels. There he met with government ministers and other associates. He returned to Laeken by 6:30 for dinner. Before bed, he read several newspapers.

This was King Leopold's routine, seven days a week. Not a minute was wasted all day. "Time is money," he liked to say.

As part of his daily routine, the king began to build a nation 4,000 miles away in Africa. He raised money to build a railway and explore the Congo Free State. He chose government officials for the country and decided how much they would be paid. He named a governor-general, who moved into a mansion in Boma. European officials ate three meals a day in the hotel there. They celebrated the king's birthday

THE CONGOLESE CHIEF MIVERO shows the buttons and medals he
was awarded for service to Leopold.

each year with a shooting contest. A choir of African children sang for the occasion.

Slowly, Leopold's agents spread out into the Congo. By 1890, they had expanded the number of stations to 50. The station chiefs each worked for Leopold's Congo Free State. They cleared land for houses. And they demanded help from the African leaders. Each tribal leader who cooperated got a medal with Leopold's image on it. On the back the medal read "Loyalty and Devotion."

But the station chiefs wanted more than just loyalty from the tribal leaders. Under orders from Leopold, they demanded ivory.

Ivory was in style in Europe at the time. Wealthy buyers paid a lot of money for ivory knife handles, pool balls, combs, chess pieces, and piano keys. The Congo quickly became a major supplier.

In the beginning, the station chiefs tried to buy elephant tusks from Congolese hunters. The white men paid in beads, cloth, and other trinkets. But

CONGOLESE MEN CARRY ELEPHANT TUSKS from the interior
to the coast. Leopold made huge profits selling ivory in Europe, but
Africans were rarely paid for their work.

when the supply ran low, they used force to get what
they wanted.

It was this system that horrified the journalist
George Washington Williams when he came to the
Congo in 1890. Williams was the first person to
publicly criticize the king of the Congo Free State.
Leopold, he charged, had tricked tribal leaders out
of their land. His agents understood nothing about

the Africans. They didn't speak the local languages. Instead they ruled with guns and whips.

Leopold responded quickly to Williams's accusations. He called his advisers to a special meeting. They contacted newspaper reporters and convinced them to attack the American personally. In the summer of 1891, the Congo Free State published a 45-page report to answer Williams's accusations.

The report seemed to satisfy Leopold's critics. A month later, Williams was dead. And people quickly forgot about his complaints.

Leopold continued to insist that his purpose in the Congo was to help the Africans. "The Congo Free State is certainly not a business," he told the prime minister of Belgium.

But in fact, that's exactly what it was. And far from helping the Africans, the Free State was turning many of them into slaves.

THE CONGOLESE

WHEN LEOPOLD TOOK OVER THE CONGO, there may have been as many as 20 million Africans living there. Most of the Congolese lived in small groups. They raised vegetables in their villages. They hunted in the forests. Groups that had contact with outsiders sold ivory and slaves to Arab or European traders.

A CONGOLESE MAN around 1900.

The Congolese weren't well equipped to take on the Europeans. Many of the tribes made beautiful artwork and metalwork. But their military technology lagged behind the Europeans' guns.

More importantly, they were not united. The Congolese belonged to 200 different ethnic groups and spoke 400 different languages.

As the stations of the Congo Free State expanded, many Africans tried to resist. Many were killed in the process. Others were forced to watch while their way of life changed forever.

CHAPTER 9

Slave State

A NEW KIND OF SLAVERY
comes to the Congo.

IN 1891, LEOPOLD'S BUSINESS IN THE CONGO was not running smoothly. It cost a lot of money to build roads and stations. Leopold was not making enough money in return.

That year, he announced a new law that would have a devastating effect on the Congolese. All natural resources in the Congo now belonged to the Congo Free State. Employees of the Free State—called agents—would pay the Congolese to collect ivory and other products for them. But the

Congolese could no longer trade with whomever they pleased.

Leopold also decided to lease parts of the country to private businesses. In those areas, the businesses would act as a government. They'd have their own police forces to enforce the law. And they too would control all trade on their land.

Villagers soon felt the change. State agents arrived in the villages with armed soldiers. They announced that each village chief had to hand over a certain amount of ivory and food each month. If the stations needed labor, the villagers had to supply that as well.

In the early years, the whites demanded plenty of labor. They wanted land cleared for stations. Station chiefs wanted house servants. Most of all, the whites wanted porters. In the lower Congo, many tons of supplies had to be carried hundreds of miles past the rapids. By the mid-1890s, the state used 50,000 porters a year.

And when they couldn't get people to work for pieces of cloth or beads, agents of the Congo Free State forced the Congolese to work. Visitors to the Congo often saw long lines of black porters chained at the neck. Children as young as seven carried heavy loads. One station developed a reputation for seizing Africans and forcing them to work. Local villagers called the station Baka Baka, which meant "capture, capture."

Agents controlled porters and other laborers with a brutal tool called the *chicotte*. The *chicotte* was a whip made out of tough hippopotamus hide. Some white officials used it to punish the smallest offense. An officer once had 30 kids whipped because he thought they had laughed at him.

The Congo Free State did have laws against this kind of brutality. But they were rarely enforced seriously enough to make a difference. One station chief beat two African servants to death in 1890. He was fined 500 francs (about $2,500 in today's money).

For the Congolese, however, the laws were harsh. And Leopold had an army to enforce them. He called it the Force Publique. Its officers were Europeans. Its soldiers came from local villages or other African countries. By 1900, nearly 20,000 soldiers were stationed at 183 posts around the country.

The Force Publique kept order in the Congo. They also made sure the ivory kept coming. Soldiers often marched into villages that weren't producing

SOLDIERS FROM THE FORCE PUBLIQUE in Boma. Under orders from white officers, they forced villagers to produce ivory and food.

ivory or food. Their officers demanded that the villagers meet their quotas. Sometimes the soldiers shot or beat people as a warning. Sometimes they captured men to use as porters and led them off at gunpoint. In some cases, rebellious villages were burned to the ground.

Local tribes stood little chance against the well-armed Force Publique. But many of them tried to rebel anyway. Late in 1893, for example, a tribal leader named Nzansu killed the station chief at Baka Baka. Nzansu's rebels blocked all people and goods from reaching Stanley Pool. It took the Force Publique eight months to stop the rebellion.

Most rebellions ended the same way. Leaders were killed. Their followers fled into the forest. Some white officers and their black soldiers committed terrible crimes in the process. The station chief at Stanley Falls put down a rebellion in 1895. He had the heads chopped off of 21 of his prisoners. Then he arranged them in his flower garden as a warning to others.

Over the years, Leopold's Force Publique put down at least 12 large rebellions and many more small ones. Despite the odds against them, the Congolese kept fighting. In the words of one tribal leader, "If we let the white men into this country, they will soon make an end of us."

C H A P T E R   1 0

Rubber Is King

A smoother ride in Europe
LEADS TO MISERY
IN AFRICA.

As LEOPOLD'S AGENTS TIGHTENED their
hold on the Congo, an event happened far away that
would change millions of lives in Africa.

In Ireland, a man named John Dunlop wanted to
find a way to give bicyclists a smoother ride. He found
a solution while working on the tires of his son's
tricycle. In 1890, he turned his idea into a business.
He started the Dunlop Company and began producing
rubber tires that inflated with air.

Dunlop's invention created a huge demand for rubber. And the Congo had one of the world's largest supplies. Rain forest covered half the country. In the forest, thick vines filled with a sticky liquid climbed high up the trees. When the vines were cut, the liquid dripped out. When the liquid hardened, it turned to rubber that could be manufactured into tires.

By the mid-1890s, agents of the Congo Free State demanded rubber as well as ivory. Each adult male Congolese had to produce between six and nine pounds every two weeks. The work was exhausting and often dangerous. Workers spent weeks at a time in the forest. They often slept in wooden cages to protect themselves from leopards. Rubber vines reached dozens of feet into the air. To get all the rubber they needed, workers had to climb. White travelers sometimes found the broken bodies of rubber-gatherers on the forest floor.

Under these conditions, many Africans weren't willing to do the work. "The native doesn't like making rubber," one white officer wrote in his diary. "He must be compelled to do it."

And that's exactly what Leopold's agents did. To force Africans to bring in rubber, they developed a brutally effective strategy. They took hostages. The Force Publique visited villages that fell behind on their rubber quotas. Since men did most of the rubber gathering, the agents usually seized women. They held the prisoners under guard at their stations. When the village collected enough rubber, the agents sent the women back.

Many state agents even had an instruction book with a section on taking hostages. "In Africa, taking prisoners is . . . an easy thing to do," the section began. Then it described exactly how to do it. When villagers fled into the forest, they always returned for food. An officer simply had to leave guards near the village garden. "You will be certain of capturing people after a brief delay," the book concluded.

By the late 1890s, business was booming for the Congo Free State. Ivory hunters had killed off nearly

AFRICANS, INCLUDING YOUNG CHILDREN, line up
with their quotas of rubber on their heads.

all the elephant herds in the country. But rubber was
even more profitable. Africans brought it into the
stations in baskets. Agents dried it into slabs in the
sun. Then they loaded it onto steamships and sent it
to Leopoldville.

At Leopoldville, workers heaved the rubber onto
railway cars. The cargo made the 260-mile trip to the

coast on Leopold's new tracks. Large cargo ships then took it to ports in Belgium. From there it was sold to factories in Europe and the United States for seven times what it cost to collect.

As the demand for rubber grew, agents of the Congo Free State put more and more pressure on the Africans. Army raids to round up workers became more and more common. By 1900, the Free State was spending half its budget on the Force Publique.

Leopold's soldiers were under orders to get results. When the Force Publique raided a village, they demanded food and laborers. They didn't hesitate to shoot anyone who resisted. They became known for their brutality throughout the Congo.

One practice was especially shocking. When Force Publique troops returned from a raid, they usually carried a basket filled with human hands, cut from their victims. Their officers liked to keep track of how many people their troops killed. They also wanted to make sure their soldiers did not waste bullets. The hands were proof that the bullets had killed their targets. When bullets were wasted, some soldiers were known to cut the hands off living victims to make it seem as though those bullets had killed people.

The Force Publique ruined lives all across the Congo. Thousands of people were forced out of their homes. One white observer had seen it happen over and over. "All the people of the villages run away to the forest when they hear the State officers are coming," he wrote. "Tonight . . . 40,000 people, men, women, children, with the sick, are sleeping in the forests without shelter."

Years later, African villagers still remembered the terror. One man, named Tswambe, recalled the raids and the severed hands. "Rubber caused these torments," he said. "That's why we no longer want to hear its name spoken."

CHAPTER 11

Voices in the Wilderness

THE KING DODGES HIS CRITICS
in the Congo.

BACK IN BELGIUM, Leopold enjoyed his control of the Congo. He imported African animals for Belgian zoos. He had the bedroom of his private railway car paneled with wood from the Congo. He added a Congo section to his greenhouse at Laeken. In it, visitors could walk among palm trees and other plants from Africa.

Leopold also used money from the Congo for building projects in Belgium and France. He built a

LEOPOLD ADDED A CONGO SECTION TO
HIS GREENHOUSE in Laeken. He had palm trees, geraniums, and
other tropical plants shipped here.

golf course and a new royal chalet. He built parks in the seaside resort of Ostend, where he often spent time. He built mansions in the south of France.

For the most part, Europeans had no idea how much violence lay behind the money coming from the Congo. But little by little, reports began to leak out.

Many of these reports came from Leopold's harshest critics in Africa: religious missionaries. These determined preachers came from England, the United States, Sweden, and other places. They left their familiar homes to live in African villages. Their goal was to convert their new neighbors to Christianity. They set up churches in grass huts. They preached on Sundays. They handed out western clothes. They taught villagers how to read and gave them Bibles to practice with.

The missionaries saw the work of Leopold's agents up close. One day, an American minister came across a chief bent over a smoldering fire. The chief's tribe was allied with the Force Publique. The man was smoking

MISSIONARIES HOPED that colonization would be good for Africans. They were outraged by the brutality of the Free State. Here, a missionary frees a group of enslaved men and boys.

human hands over the fire to keep them from rotting. "See! Here is our evidence," the chief said. "I always have to cut off the right hands . . . to show the state how many we kill."

In 1895, an American Baptist missionary named John Murphy went to the British newspapers with stories from the Congo. He told about the hostages and the severed hands. The state agents had unlimited power over the Africans, he said. "If the people do not . . . rebel," he said, "it is because they are in despair."

As the reports added up, Leopold had to respond. Publicly, he said he was shocked. He also claimed that the abuses were unusual. It was impossible to control everyone who worked for the Congo Free State. Perhaps there were a few bad people who abused their power. If so, he would find them and put a stop to it.

In 1896, the king formed a Commission for the Protection of the Natives. The group had six members, all of them missionaries. Their job was to look into reports of crimes in the Congo.

Leopold won high praise for forming the commission. One newspaper said he had "faced the facts of the situation."

The commission, however, never found many facts at all. Its members lived in areas that were relatively peaceful. Leopold gave them no money to travel. They had no power to publish reports or to change policy in the Congo. In the end they met only twice. Each time only half the members showed up.

For now, Leopold had escaped his critics. In 1897, he was proud to host a World's Fair in Brussels. The colony he had worked so hard to obtain was the subject of one of the most popular exhibits. At least a million people came to see it. For their enjoyment, Leopold brought 267 people from the Congo to Brussels. The Africans lived in three specially built villages. They danced and paddled canoes around a pond while European visitors watched. In one of the villages, 90 Force Publique soldiers marched and drilled. Some of the soldiers played music in a military band.

To the fair's white visitors, the Congolese seemed strange and exotic. Some people wondered if the Africans were dangerous. Other observers simply looked on in fascination. Few people thought it was strange that human beings were being kept like animals in a zoo. Fewer still knew much about the lives of the Congolese back at home.

Thanks to the efforts of a man named Edmund Morel, that was about to change.

Leopold II in Pictures

RAISED IN A PALACE
Leopold grew up here, in a palace outside of Brussels, Belgium. The young prince had to make appointments to see his father.

PRINCE LEOPOLD
Leopold was an awkward young man, but his father thought he was "sly" like a fox.

UNEXPLORED BY EUROPEANS
In 1872, when this map was made, large sections of Africa still had not been explored by Europeans. Leopold saw this as his best chance to acquire a colony.

ACROSS AFRICA
In 1874, explorer Henry Morton Stanley embarked on an expedition to follow the Congo River to the sea. He traveled 7,000 miles in 999 days.

THE EXPLORER
Stanley made two widely publicized expeditions into Africa. Leopold avidly followed his adventures.

ROUGH SAILING
Stanley reported that the Congo River was a "great highway." However, in many areas, rapids and waterfalls made the river impossible to navigate.

LEOPOLD SEIZES CONTROL

In 1884, Leopold took control over central Africa, which he named the Congo Free State. He organized the Force Publique, an army of African soldiers, to force villagers into producing food, ivory, and rubber.

SLAVES TO RUBBER

Congolese workers beat rubber to remove pieces of wood and fiber. The invention of inflatable rubber tires in 1890 increased the misery of Africans. Millions died trying to harvest the rubber demanded by Europeans.

LEOPOLD'S SLAVE STATE

Two African overseers present a group of Congolese slaves chained at the neck. Leopold claimed that his goal was to end slavery in the Congo. In fact, he used forced labor to build his colony.

A COSTLY MONUMENT

Leopold paid for this monument in Brussels with profits from the Congo earned with the help of slave labor. Some called it the "Arc of the Severed Hands."

ENSLAVED

A Congolese prisoner handcuffed and tied up in a net.

AN OUTSPOKEN CRITIC

George Washington Williams, a journalist and veteran of the U.S. Civil War, was the first to criticize Leopold's reign in the Congo.

A PRINCIPLED WHISTLE-BLOWER

Edmund Morel worked for a shipping company that brought cargo to and from the Congo. He launched a crusade against Leopold after he began to suspect that the king was using slave labor in the Congo.

A HOLY MISSION

A missionary to the Congo stands with his students. Many missionaries were disillusioned to find that Leopold had little interest in fighting slavery or building hospitals and schools.

THE EVIDENCE

Activists from Morel's Congo Reform Association held public meetings to expose Leopold's system of forced labor. They often displayed evidence like this whip, called a *chicotte*. Made of tough hippo hide, it was used by Leopold's agents in the Congo.

A WAY OF LIFE DESTROYED

In 1906, Leopold agreed to transfer ownership of the Congo to Belgium. There is no way to calculate the number of lives that had been destroyed during the 24 years of his reign.

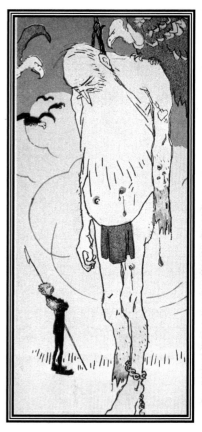

PUBLIC OPINION TURNS

Inspired by Morel and other activists, newspapers began to criticize Leopold. In this newspaper cartoon, an artist imagines Leopold getting the same punishments his agents gave thousands of Congolese people.

PART 3

Fall
of a
King

The Awakening

Leopold gets
A WORTHY ADVERSARY.

EDMUND MOREL, LIKE KING LEOPOLD, had never been to Africa. But few people were in a better position to learn the secrets of the Congo. Morel was in charge of the Congo department of a shipping company called Elder Dempster. And Elder Dempster controlled all the shipping to and from the Congo.

Not long after Leopold's World's Fair, Morel began to notice something alarming about the cargoes leaving Belgium for the Congo. Ship after ship left the docks filled only with arms and ammunition. And

Leopold's aides insisted that the contents of the ships not be made public.

Morel decided to investigate. After work each night he studied Elder Dempster's shipping records. He took careful notes. He made calculations. And he began to understand the dirty secret behind Leopold's colony: It was using slave labor.

Every year, the Congo shipped out huge amounts of rubber and ivory. By 1900, 11 million tons of rubber left Leopoldville each year. Thousands of Africans must have been working long hours to collect that much rubber. But while the ships returning to the Congo were full of military supplies, they carried very little cloth and other goods used to pay laborers. How then were the African workers getting paid?

Morel was shocked by his own conclusion. For the most part, he decided, the workers weren't getting paid at all. The Congo was being robbed. Its African laborers were little more than slaves. "I had stumbled upon a secret society of murderers," he wrote. And the king of Belgium was in charge of the killings.

Morel went to his boss with his findings. His boss immediately left to meet with King Leopold. He returned to say that the king was working hard to change the way the Congo did business. Then the boss offered Morel money to transfer to another country.

But Morel wouldn't turn back. In 1901, he quit his job. He was 28. He had almost no money and a family to support. But he was determined to "expose and destroy" Leopold's regime in the Congo.

Leopold could not have had a more determined adversary. Morel gathered all the information he could on the Congo. He traveled the world to raise money for his cause. And he began to write. In 1903 he started his own publication, the *West African Mail*. He wrote books, articles, pamphlets, and letters to newspapers around the world.

Leopold refused to let Morel enter the Congo. But as Morel's reputation spread, people came to him with information. Missionaries sent him photographs of whippings and boys whose hands had been cut off. Force Publique officers sent him secret documents. He reported on the practice of taking hostages. He even printed lists of the dead:

1. Bokangu, Chief, Killed with blows with butt of gun
2. Mangundwa " " " " " " " "
3. Ekunga " " " " " " " " "

EDMUND MOREL, a clerk from a shipping company, quit his job to "expose and destroy" Leopold's exploitation of the Congolese.

Morel's tireless efforts began to make a difference. The violence in the Congo made the front pages of the newspapers. In the spring of 1903, the English parliament called for an investigation. The British sent a message to their representative, or consul, in the Congo. He was to travel up the Congo and "send reports soon."

At Laeken, Leopold began to squirm under pressure from Morel. The king had his spokesmen respond to the attacks. They admitted that there had probably been abuses. But they denied that the Congo Free State had approved them. It was not official policy to take hostages, they insisted.

Morel responded by printing the form used by company agents to list the hostages they had taken.

Morel's attacks had Leopold on the defensive. According to Morel, the king even tried to bribe him. Morel's old boss invited Morel to a dinner party in London. A Belgian shipping executive introduced himself as a representative of the king. The executive suggested that Morel might benefit if he stopped attacking the Free State government. He hinted quietly that things could be done to help Morel and his family. "Everything could be arranged," the man said.

Morel left the meeting amused at Leopold's boldness. Much to the king's frustration, his adversary could not be bought.

The Casement Report

The eyes of the world
ARE WATCHING THE CONGO.

AT HOME IN LAEKEN, KING LEOPOLD'S evenings could not have been peaceful. Every night after dinner, he settled in to read the newspapers. And the news was rarely good. If the Congo didn't make the paper, the king's personal life often did.

Around 1900, Leopold met a young French woman named Caroline Delacroix. He was 65; she was not yet 20. But the king began to see her regularly when he went to Paris. Soon the two started traveling together. Caroline even appeared at official events with the king. In 1901, Leopold brought her to the funeral of his cousin, Queen Victoria of England.

In 1903, the king's wife died. She had spent the last years of her life reading about her husband and his mistress in the newspapers. With Marie-Henriette gone, Leopold moved Caroline into a mansion across the street from the palace at Laeken. He built a bridge over the road so she could visit with ease.

By this time, Leopold's two eldest daughters hated him. He had married both girls to Austrian princes when they were teenagers. Louise had a public affair with an army officer. She asked her father for help in getting a divorce. When he refused, she ran away with the army officer. Stephanie's marriage had also been miserable from the start. In 1889, her husband committed suicide with his mistress. In 1901, Stephanie remarried without asking for her father's approval.

Leopold stopped speaking to both daughters. He also tried to avoid leaving them money in his will. Belgian law required parents to leave their possessions to their children. Leopold spent years lobbying Parliament to change the law.

But at the beginning of 1904, the Congo was the king's main concern. The British consul had just returned from his fact-finding trip up the Congo. And his report was not good.

The consul was a man named Roger Casement. He had worked in Africa on and off for 20 years, since he was 18. But he hadn't traveled widely in the Congo and didn't realize how bad things were.

On the fact-finding trip, Casement spent three and a half months in the heart of the Congo. He saw for himself the effects of the forced labor system. Everywhere he went, Africans had horror stories to tell. In one place he met five people who had hiked for miles to meet him. Thanks to the Force Publique, each of his visitors had no right hand. In another place, Casement wrote in his diary, "The country a desert, no natives left."

Casement estimated that the population had dropped by 60 percent in some parts of the Congo. Disease was everywhere. So were the graves of villagers killed by the Force Publique. He also met many women who were refusing to have children. According to Casement, they wanted to be able to run from the soldiers.

Casement returned to Boma tired and angry. He wrote to the Free State's governor-general. "The system is bad," he said, "hopelessly and entirely bad."

Leopold tried his best to keep the British from making the report public. But in February 1904, the report came out. Edmund Morel, for one, was thrilled. Finally, he wrote, someone had exposed "the most gigantic fraud and wickedness which our generation has known."

By this time, Casement had returned to Europe. He went to visit Morel in England. The two men instantly became friends. They stayed up until 2:00 A.M. talking about the Congo. Morel listened in horror to Casement's stories. And they decided to work together to end Leopold's rule in the Congo. Casement wrote Morel a check for 100 British pounds. Morel bought a typewriter and a few other supplies. And the Congo Reform Association was born.

Morel dug into his work like never before. He sometimes spent 18 hours at a time in his office. He wrote letter after letter. He published his weekly newspaper. He got missionaries from the Congo to go on tour and speak to groups of people. One reverend and his wife brought along *chicottes* and shackles when they spoke. Morel himself organized mass meetings in lecture halls. He showed slides of whipping victims and severed hands. Often the crowd would yell "Shame! Shame!"

There were plenty of villains in the Congo. But to Morel and the other activists, Leopold II was the king of them all. Before long, cartoons appeared in

THIS POLITICAL CARTOON FROM GERMANY showed Leopold surrounded by heads of his Congolese victims. Leopold had hoped that colonization would bring glory to Belgium. Instead, public opinion was turning against him.

the newspapers portraying Leopold as a monster. One showed the king with blood dripping from his long white beard. Another had him eating body parts for dinner. Furious with his critics, Leopold canceled his subscription to his favorite newspaper, the *Times* of London.

CHAPTER 14

A Losing Battle

THE KING TRIES DESPERATELY
to hang onto his colony.

IN MARCH 1904, LEOPOLD RESPONDED to the Casement report. He sent out a 37-page note answering the charges in detail. He claimed that Casement had gotten his information from "untruthful" Africans and "biased" missionaries. He insisted that the Congolese were dying from disease, not murder. As for the forced labor, he said it was the only way to get Africans to work. In the long run, he claimed, it would teach them how to get along in a modern society.

AFTER HIS REPORT CAME OUT, Roger Casement was attacked by Leopold. The King of England gave him a medal and Casement later said that his work in the Congo was the best thing he had ever done.

Leopold then spent 17 pages on the case of a boy who had lost his hand to the Force Publique. The boy had not in fact had his hand cut off, Leopold said. It had been bitten off by a wild boar.

Leopold also organized a public relations office to defend the Free State. The new group started newspapers. It published pamphlets with titles like, "The Congo State Is NOT a Slave State." It bribed newspaper editors to keep Morel's stories out of their papers. It steered critical journalists away from problem areas in the Congo. It also paid its own journalists to go to the Congo and find stories that made the Free State look good. One station agent was told to prepare for a visit from one of these reporters by tearing down a jail.

But it was too late to hide the crimes of the Free State. Thanks to Edmund Morel, the world was watching. Every week, it seemed, a new celebrity joined the Congo Reform Association. Its members included a Polish prince and a famous French novelist. The American writer Mark Twain joined. So did African-American leader Booker T. Washington.

Under fire from all sides, Leopold agreed to start another investigation. He named three judges to a Commission of Inquiry. In October 1904, the judges arrived in Boma. Like Casement, they spent four months steaming up the Congo. On the boat and in station huts, they interviewed 370 people. One of their informants was a tribal chief named Lontulu. The chief came in and laid a line of twigs on the table. There were 110 of them, he said, one for each member of his tribe killed by the state.

The judges returned to Boma in March. They told the Free State's governor-general about their findings. The governor confessed that it was all true. The forced labor, the hostages, the raids; it was all government policy, he said. Then he committed suicide.

The commission's report came out in November 1905. The story it told was already a familiar one. But now, no one could blame it on the missionaries or the Africans. This report came from judges appointed by the king himself.

For Leopold, it was the final blow. The Belgian people, by this time, were fed up with him. Leopold and his colony were an embarrassment to Belgium, they felt.

Leopold was in the south of France when the commission's report came out. He spent his vacations there now. On the French Riviera, he could escape it all. He lived on the most expensive property in the world. He worked on his yacht. Caroline Delacroix had a home there as well.

By the end of 1906, the king was tired of fighting. The British demanded that he hand over the Congo to Belgium. His own aides agreed. In December, Leopold finally gave in. He told his prime minister to begin transferring the Congo to Belgian rule. "[The Belgian people] are tired of me," he grumbled. "They want no more of me."

CHAPTER 15

End of the King Sovereign

NEAR THE END OF HIS LIFE, Leopold loses the colony he had ruled for 23 years.

IN 1907, THE KING OF BELGIUM TURNED 72. He spent more and more time in France with Caroline Delacroix. The two of them now had two sons together. But they still did not officially live together. He traveled to visit her through an underground passage. Leopold liked everything "secret and mysterious," she said.

In fact, the king had developed some strange habits over the years. He rode around the grounds at Laeken on a huge tricycle. Leopold was terrified of disease and did everything he could to keep from getting sick. He drank huge amounts of warm water because he thought it was good for his health. He had his newspapers ironed every day to get rid of the germs.

AS HE AGED, LEOPOLD II became even more eccentric and isolated. He acknowledged that even his own people "are tired of me."

He often sent his aides away if they sneezed in his presence. When Caroline needed some time to herself, she simply had to cough a few times. That was enough to get her banished from Leopold's company.

In Leopold's final years, he planned massive building projects. He spent his time traveling from one to the other, watching and supervising. He planned a huge spa in the south of France. He wandered in the ever-expanding greenhouses at Laeken. In Brussels, he had a special platform built so he could watch a building go up near his office. Finally, there was a huge stone archway in the center of Brussels, built with money from the Congo. Some Belgians referred to it as the "Arc of the Severed Hands."

In November 1908, the residents of Boma gathered for a ceremony. Belgium officially took over the Congo from Leopold.

The next fall, the Belgian government announced some changes in the Congo. Africans would be allowed to gather rubber, ivory, and other products freely.

They could not be forced to trade with anyone. People would pay their taxes in money. The government could no longer force people to work.

In reality, the changes did not make life a lot better for the Congolese. Most of the land in the Congo still belonged to the government or to private companies. Africans had to make money to pay taxes. Their only choice was to go to work for the Belgians in mines or on large-scale farms.

Leopold did not live to see much of the new Congo. In December 1909 he got sick, probably with cancer. He and Caroline were quickly married by a priest. Leopold's daughters returned to Brussels, but the king refused to see them. Doctors tried to operate on him, but the former King Sovereign of the Congo died the following day. Caroline was led from the room, weeping.

When Caroline tried to get into her home in Brussels, she found that the locks had been changed. Louise and Stephanie had already begun a battle over the king's estate.

It took years for the Belgian government to sort out the king's finances. Leopold had always claimed that he didn't make money from the Congo. "Is it not wretched to have been the king of this state for 22 years and to have kept nothing for oneself?" he once complained.

But in fact the king had hidden millions of francs in secret companies and foundations. One of these companies owned 58 properties in Brussels. Another held 45 million francs' worth of paintings and other valuables. In 24 years as ruler of the Congo, the king probably made about 220 million francs. That amounts to $1.1 billion in today's money. No one is sure of the exact figure, however. The king had all of the Congo's financial records destroyed just before he died.

No record remained, either, of the exact number of lives destroyed in the Congo during the previous 24 years.

The Scramble for Africa

In 1884, just before Leopold II acquired the Congo Free State, most of Africa was owned by Africans.

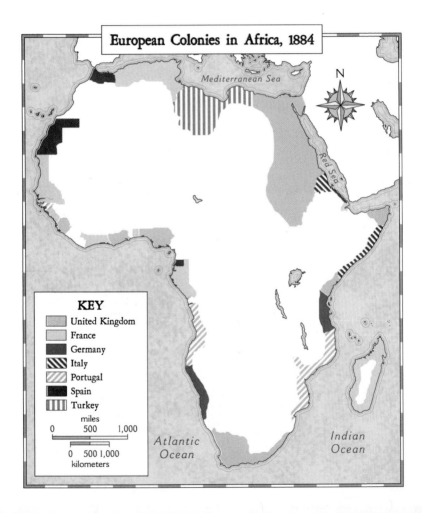

European Colonies in Africa, 1884

N

Mediterranean Sea

Red Sea

KEY
- United Kingdom
- France
- Germany
- Italy
- Portugal
- Spain
- Turkey

miles
0   500   1,000

0   500 1,000
kilometers

Atlantic Ocean

Indian Ocean

But within 30 years, European countries had taken over almost the entire continent.

Not until the 1950s would African nations begin to win their independence.

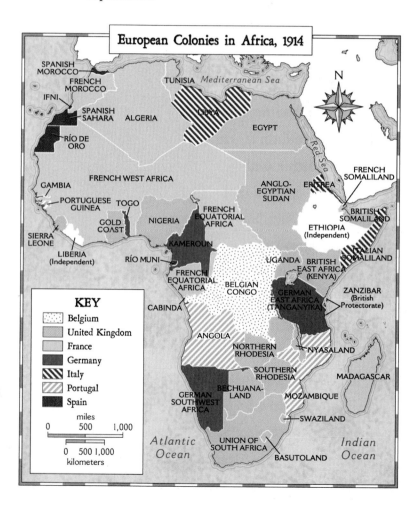

European Colonies in Africa, 1914

SPANISH MOROCCO
FRENCH MOROCCO
IFNI
SPANISH SAHARA
ALGERIA
TUNISIA
Mediterranean Sea
LIBYA
EGYPT
RÍO DE ORO
N
FRENCH SOMALILAND
GAMBIA
FRENCH WEST AFRICA
ANGLO-EGYPTIAN SUDAN
ERITREA
PORTUGUESE GUINEA
TOGO
GOLD COAST
NIGERIA
FRENCH EQUATORIAL AFRICA
BRITISH SOMALILAND
SIERRA LEONE
LIBERIA (Independent)
KAMEROUN
RÍO MUNI
ETHIOPIA (Independent)
ITALIAN SOMALILAND
FRENCH EQUATORIAL AFRICA
BELGIAN CONGO
UGANDA
BRITISH EAST AFRICA (KENYA)
CABINDA
GERMAN EAST AFRICA (TANGANYIKA)
ZANZIBAR (British Protectorate)
ANGOLA
NORTHERN RHODESIA
NYASALAND
SOUTHERN RHODESIA
MADAGASCAR
GERMAN SOUTHWEST AFRICA
BECHUANA-LAND
MOZAMBIQUE
SWAZILAND
UNION OF SOUTH AFRICA
BASUTOLAND
Red Sea
Atlantic Ocean
Indian Ocean

KEY
Belgium
United Kingdom
France
Germany
Italy
Portugal
Spain

miles
0   500   1,000

0 500 1,000
kilometers

Wicked?

What damage did Leopold II do to the Congo during his 24-year reign? In 1919, the Belgian government decided to find out.

According to the government's report, the Congo's population had been cut in half since 1880. Ten million people had either died or left the Congo in 40 years.

Leopold and his agents cannot be blamed for all of these deaths. The king claimed that many people had died from disease. He was right. In 1901 alone, a disease called sleeping sickness killed 500,000 people in the Congo. Thousands died from smallpox as well.

It's impossible to say how many people were killed by the forced labor system and the rifles of the Force Publique. What's clear is that the Europeans destroyed a way of life. Under Free State rule, most Africans no longer supported themselves independently. Men were forced to work as porters.

They had to collect ivory or rubber. They had to produce food for the Europeans.

To impose this new system, the Free State used violence. Its soldiers killed thousands of people. They whipped and beat thousands more. They destroyed hundreds of villages.

King Leopold, of course, did not commit any of these crimes personally. He never set foot in the Congo. The closest he ever got to a living African was probably at the World's Fair in Brussels.

But it's safe to say that Leopold knew what was happening. The Congo was his life's work. And he went about it with great attention to detail. As the Congo's king, he was responsible for the way the colony was run. Leopold set goals for the amount of rubber and ivory the colony had to produce. In order to meet those goals, his agents had to force Africans into hard labor.

Along the way, Leopold had plenty of chances to change the way his people did business in the Congo.

George Washington Williams, the missionaries, and finally Morel and Casement, made it clear what was happening there. Each time the king responded with a public relations campaign, not with real reforms.

Like many Europeans at the time, the king chose to lie to himself and others about what was happening in Africa. He insisted that Africans would benefit from colonial rule. They would learn to work and make money in a modern economy. They might even learn to govern themselves. In the meantime, he said, forced labor was the "only way to civilize and uplift" people like the Congolese.

Leopold's understanding of the Congo and its people never went any further. As a British diplomat once said, the king was too busy thinking of how he could "squeeze money out of the people."

In getting money out of the Congo, Leopold created a system more brutal than anything that had existed there before. A Swedish missionary in the Congo had the same thought while watching

Leopold's agents at work. "It is strange," he wrote, "that people who claim to be civilized think they can treat their fellow man . . . any which way."

Timeline of Terror

1835

1850: Queen Louise-Marie of Orléans, the mother of Leopold, dies.

1853: Leopold marries Marie-Henriette of Austria.

1865: King Leopold I dies; his son becomes Leopold II.

1874: Explorer Henry Morton Stanley starts his mission to cross Africa from east to west.

1876: Leopold organizes the Geographical Conference in Brussels to convince leaders of his humanitarian vision for the Congo.

1878: Leopold hires Stanley to begin building his colony in the Congo.

1884: At the Berlin Conference, the major powers of Europe give Leopold II control over the Congo. He names his colony the Congo Free State.

1890: U.S. journalist George Washington Williams visits the Congo and becomes Leopold's first public critic.

1891: Leopold announces that all resources in the Congo Free State belong to its government.

mid-1890s: Rubber trade surpasses ivory, imposing brutal new hardships on the Congolese.

1895: Baptist missionary John Murphy reports on abuses in the Congo.

1901: Edmund Morel quits his job to "expose and destroy" Leopold's regime in the Congo.

1903: The English parliament calls for an investigation of the Congo. Roger Casement releases his damning report the following year.

1904: Morel and Casement form the Congo Reform Association.

1906: Leopold agrees to hand the Congo over to Belgium.

1909

GLOSSARY

abuse (uh-BYOOSS) *noun* wrong or harmful treatment of someone

adversary (AD-ver-sehr-ee) *noun* someone who fights or argues against you

artisan (AR-tuh-zuhn) *noun* someone who is skilled at working with his or her hands at a particular craft

chicotte (shih-COT) *noun* a whip made of raw hippopotamus hide cut in a corkscrew fashion to give it sharp edges; it was used against Congolese workers during the reign of Leopold II

civilization (siv-i-luh-ZAY-shuhn) *noun* a highly developed and organized society

colony (KOL-uh-nee) *noun* a territory that has been settled by people from another country and is controlled by that country

commerce (COM-urss) *noun* the buying and selling of things in order to make money

consul (KON-suhl) *noun* someone appointed by the government of a country to live in another country or territory and protect fellow citizens who are working or traveling abroad

devastating (DEV-uh-stay-ting) *adjective* causing great distress, damage, or destruction

empire (EM-pire) *noun* a group of countries that have the same ruler

Force Publique (fohrss poo-BLEEK) *noun* the official armed force in the Congo during Leopold's rule; made up of white Belgian officers and African soldiers, its aim was to terrorize the local people

khedive (keh-DEEV) *noun* a ruler of Egypt from 1867 to 1914 who governed as a representative of the sultan of Turkey

lease (LEESS) *verb* to rent land or property to another for a specified time and a specified amount of money

merchant ship (MUR-chuhnt SHIP) *noun* a ship that carries goods for trade

missionary (MISH-uh-ner-ee) *noun* someone who is sent by a religious group to another place to teach that group's faith and do good works

parliament (PAR-luh-muhnt) *noun* the group of people who have been elected to make laws in some countries, such as Belgium and the United Kingdom

porter (POR-tur) *noun* someone hired to transport things during a journey

pound (POUND) *noun* a unit of money used in England

province (PROV-uhnss) *noun* a district or region of some countries

sleeping sickness (SLEE-ping SIK-ness) *noun* a serious disease common in much of tropical Africa; it is transmitted by the tsetse fly and is marked by fever, sleepiness, and shakiness

smallpox (SMAWL-poks) *noun* a serious, very contagious disease that causes high fever and skin eruptions that can leave permanent scars

sovereign (SOV-ruhn) *noun* supreme leader of a nation or territory

stations (STAY-shuhns) *noun* small military settlements set up along the Congo River during King Leopold II's rule; each station had a few thatched-roof huts

station chief (STAY-shun CHEEF) *noun* the white official in charge of a station in the Congo

statistic (stuh-TISS-tik) *noun* a fact or piece of information expressed as a number or percentage

sultan (SUHLT-uhn) *noun* a king or ruler of some Muslim countries

FIND OUT MORE

Here are some books and Web sites with more information about Leopold II and his times.

BOOKS

Barter, James. **The Congo (Rivers of the World)**. San Diego, Lucent Books, 2003. (96 pages) *Tells about the Congo River and its relationship to the history of central Africa.*

Davenport, John. **A Brief Political and Geographical History of Africa: Where Are the Belgian Congo, Rhodesia, and Kush? (Place in Time: A Kid's Historical Guide to the Changing Names and Places of the World)**. Hockessin, DE: Mitchell Lane Publishers, 2008. (96 pages) *Discusses the history of political change on the continent of Africa.*

Fish, Bruce, and Becky Durost Fish. **The Congo: Exploration, Reform, and a Brutal Legacy (Exploration of Africa)**. Philadelphia: Chelsea House, 2000. (112 pages) *A look at the tragic history of colonialism in the Congo region.*

Willis, Terri. **Democratic Republic of the Congo (Enchantment of the World, Second Series)**. New York, Children's Press, 2004. (114 pages) *Describes the history, geography, and culture of the Democratic Republic of the Congo, the nation once known as the Congo Free State.*

Worth, Richard. **Stanley and Livingston and the Exploration of Africa in World History**. Berkeley Heights, NJ: Enslow, 2000. (128 pages) *Follows the explorations of Stanley and Livingston as they unlock many geographic secrets in Africa and traces the history of European colonialism on the African continent.*

WEB SITES

http://encarta.msn.com/encyclopedia_761595444/Scramble_for_Africa.html
MSN Encarta's online encyclopedia article about the Scramble for Africa.

http://www.bbc.co.uk/worldservice/africa/features/storyofafrica/index.shtml
This BBC World Service site, called The Story of Africa, tells the history of the continent from an African perspective.

http://www.smithsonianmagazine.com/issues/2003/october/livingstone.php
This online article from Smithsonian Magazine tells how Stanley's quest to find Livingstone was also a story of newfound fascination with Africa.

For Grolier subscribers:
http://go.grolier.com/ searches: Congo, Democratic Republic of; Leopold II, King of the Belgians; Stanley, Sir Henry Morton; Casement, Sir Roger

INDEX

AUTHOR'S NOTE AND BIBLIOGRAPHY

To me, the real tragedy of Leopold's life is not greed or cruelty. It's the complete lack of empathy and understanding he had for the people of an entire continent.

The King of the Belgians couldn't have lived a more different existence from the Congolese. Leopold grew up in a palace; they grew up in grass-and-mud huts. He had more money than he could ever spend; they considered a few bolts of cloth to be a great fortune. He traveled in yachts; they paddled dugout canoes.

Leopold was never able to see the Africans he ruled as fully human. That became apparent to me when I read about the Brussels World's Fair, where the king had human beings put on display like animals in a zoo.

Of course, Leopold wasn't alone in his attitude toward the Africans. Few of the visitors to the World's Fair found the Congolese exhibit at all offensive. The difference? None of them had the power to impose their will on a land full of millions of people.

Here are the sources that were most important to me in researching Leopold's story:

Emerson, Barbara. **Leopold II of the Belgians: King of Colonialism.** New York: St. Martin's Press, 1979.

Ewans, Martin, Sir. **European Atrocity, African Catastrophe: Leopold II, the Congo Free State and its Aftermath.** London: Routledge Curzon, 2002.

Hibbert, Christopher. **Africa Explored: Europeans in the Dark Continent, 1769–1889.** New York: Norton, 1983.

Hochschild, Adam. **King Leopold's Ghost.** New York: Houghton-Mifflin, 1998.

Martelli, George. **Leopold to Lumumba, a History of the Belgian Congo, 1877–1960.** London: Chapman and Hall, 1962.

Slade, Ruth M. **King Leopold's Congo.** London: Oxford University Press, 1962.

Stanley, Henry Morton. **Congo and the Founding of its Free State.** New York: Harper and Brothers, 1885.

—Tod Olson